Juliana Deoldoto Paulino

Brothers Grimm

AF524441

Juliana Deoldoto Paulino

Brothers Grimm

A possibility for teaching and learning

ScienciaScripts

Imprint

Any brand names and product names mentioned in this book are subject to trademark, brand or patent protection and are trademarks or registered trademarks of their respective holders. The use of brand names, product names, common names, trade names, product descriptions etc. even without a particular marking in this work is in no way to be construed to mean that such names may be regarded as unrestricted in respect of trademark and brand protection legislation and could thus be used by anyone.

Cover image: www.ingimage.com

This book is a translation from the original published under ISBN 978-3-330-99890-2.

Publisher:
Sciencia Scripts
is a trademark of
Dodo Books Indian Ocean Ltd. and OmniScriptum S.R.L publishing group

120 High Road, East Finchley, London, N2 9ED, United Kingdom
Str. Armeneasca 28/1, office 1, Chisinau MD-2012, Republic of Moldova, Europe
Printed at: see last page
ISBN: 978-620-8-20836-3

Copyright © Juliana Deoldoto Paulino
Copyright © 2024 Dodo Books Indian Ocean Ltd. and OmniScriptum S.R.L publishing group

DEDICATION

To Marta Chaves, dear organized advisor and defender of a charming and excellent education.

To GEEI, my dear Research and Study Group in Early Childhood Education.

To Luzia Aparecida Deoldoto Paulino, Devanir Paulino and Marco Aurelio Deoldoto Paulino, unique parents and wonderful brother whom I love more than anything.

To Carlos UbialliNeto, my understanding boyfriend and friend at all times.

ACKNOWLEDGMENTS

Now that another stage has been completed, it's time to thank those who supported me, consoled me, encouraged me, cheered me on and contributed in one way or another to the completion of this work. With great affection, I thank you:To God, who gave me the strength to go on many times;

To my teacher and advisor Dr. Marta Chaves, one of the most incredible people I have ever met. Thank you for teaching me so much wisdom, in which we advocate an education for children that is full of enchantment. Thank you also for your care, rigor and understanding during this journey and for contributing immensely to my academic and personal growth;

To the teachers of the Pedagogy course at this University, for their teachings. In particular, to the professors on the examining board, Prof. Vimcius Stein and Prof. Ms. Luciana Grandini Cabreira, for having so kindly accepted our work. Luciana Grandini Cabreira, for having warmly accepted our invitation;

To the Research and Study Group in Early Childhood Education (GEEI), which, under the guidance of Prof. Dr.ª Marta Chaves, had a very significant impact on my education; and to its members who welcomed me with affection and shared many joys;

My dear colleague AngelaArten-Meyer, who is in Germany and helped me immensely with the images about the Brothers Grimm. My friends GessicaKeislynVolpato, Ellen Rojo and LeniaraKlering, friendships that began during my degree course, but that will last for a long time to come; the contribution of each one and everything we've been through together will never be forgotten;

To my dear friends GiovannaLaraniaga Martins, GabrielaLaraniaga Quintanilha, Rebeca Izabella Plaza Marques and Mariana Martinez, Gabriel Schincariol, Eduardo

Salvalagio, Gustavo Henrique Conceigao, Lucas El Taki Penteado da Silva, Luiz Henrique Martins and Victor Hugo Sorianip for all the help they gave me at all times, as well as their friendship;

To my dear friend Tamires FabroFavine, whose friendship will always be unique, even if it's far away. Dear "work" friends GlaciCorazza, RenataMarcomine, and SoniaMassignaniBrussolo, you were indispensable at various times when I needed help;

To my future mother-in-law, Lourdes Rodrigues, for her encouragement, ideas, affection and many collaborations along the way;

To my brother Marco Aurelio Deoldoto Paulino, who in his own way listened to my countless ideas for this work;

To my future brothers-in-law Mariana R. Ubialli and AlexandreBetioli, always helpful and friendly;

To my beloved parents, Luzia Aparecida Deoldoto Paulino and Devanir Paulino, who throughout these years of my degree simply supported me, helped me, dried my tears in difficult times and constantly encouraged me;

To my dear boyfriend Carlos UbialliNeto, who has always been a friend, companion, understanding, patient and kind, who has been able to help me by providing motivation and sharing my feelings, difficulties, expectations and dreams.

"It is true that with the passage of time tales are always renewed, but that is why their roots must be very old [...]. The epic basis of popular poetry resembles the green that spreads throughout nature in multiple gradations, that satisfies and soothes, without ever tiring.

Jacob and Wibhelm Qrimm

SUMMARY

The aim of this study is to reflect on how Children's Literature has been presented in school educational institutions, especially in Early Childhood Education and the initial years of Primary School, as experienced during the Supervised Curricular Internship in the Pedagogy course. We also intend to present a proposal for a pedagogical resource called Box of Charms and Life, based on the biography of the Brothers Grimm. This work is bibliographical in nature, based on the authors of the Historical-Cultural Theory to support our discussions, as we consider that its assumptions answer our questions. We consider it important to relate the historical aspects of Germany between the 18th and 19th centuries to the experiences of Jacob and Wilhelm Grimm and to emphasize that the more enriching experiences children can have, the richer their learning will be. In order to better understand what Children's Literature is and how to work with it in Early Childhood Education, we have first organized the historical aspects of Children's Literature, then described the research into 18th and 19th century Germany, as well as presenting some biographical aspects of the Brothers Grimm and ending with the writings on the possibility of pedagogical intervention with the didactic resource mentioned.

Keywords: Children's Literature; Grimm Brothers; Historical-Cultural Theory; Early Childhood Education.

SUMMARY

1. INTRODUCTION

The aim of this paper is to present initial studies and reflections on the Brothers Grimm's Children's Literature and its contributions to pedagogical work in Early Childhood Education. It is possible to consider that, in many school institutes, work with literature and other teaching resources that can favor and enrich learning and the relationship with a cultural universe is precarious. Problems are found such as fragmented readings of tales from Children's Literature, a shortage of books containing the names of the original authors, classrooms with no organized space for reading and a lack of organization that favours learning from the perspective of valuing art as the starting point for pedagogical interventions.

Based on the observations made during the Supervised Curricular Internship in Early Childhood and Elementary Education, which is part of the Pedagogy course curriculum, it was possible to observe the routine of the school institutions where we did our internship, as well as the pedagogical interventions carried out by teachers in the classroom.

Through the Supervised Curricular Internships and our work with the children, we noticed that they knew little about the authors of Children's Literature and their stories. When the teachers presented stories from Children's Literature, they simply told the story in part, not presenting the story in great detail, much less talking about the author of that work.We also noticed a lack of appropriate material, i.e. few copies of Children's Literature books, books without covers or missing pages, lack of work with exponents of Children's Literature, in short, we observed that these school institutes lack materials and resources that motivate children and develop their curiosity for Literature. We also noticed that the work with literature was secondary, as the teachers only worked with literature, be it through stories, poetry or music, at the end of the school term or during breaks from an activity. In dialogue with the teachers, they questioned how the interventions could be conducted, so we tried to answer a few questions: What is Children's Literature and how can we work with it in schools?

In addition to these experiences gained in school educational institutions, the experiences and studies carried out since 2011, due to joining the Research and Studies Group in Children's Education - GEEI[1] , have also been important in this journey, as they have helped us to perceive, understand and identify opportunities to develop work with Children's Literature through teaching resources and teaching strategies that allow children to have access to the cultural goods historically produced by humanity, as Leontiev (1979) writes.

Based on the observations and experiences of the aforementioned studies, the need arose to create alternatives for carrying out this work with literature and its authors in nursery and primary schools, looking for strategies on what could be done to improve students' learning.

In order to carry out these initial studies, we relied on the Science of History, the theoretical-methodological framework that underpins Historical-Cultural Theory, and on the classic authors of this theory, such as Leontiev (1979) and Vygotsky (2009), essential exponents for the defense of an educational practice that strives to present subjects with what is most elaborate in science and the arts. We also looked to scholars of Children's Literature, such as Abramovich (1989), Meireles (1984) and Coelho (2010), for important reflections on Classical Children's Literature. We emphasize the importance of Children's Literature and its threefold contribution to school work. This means that Children's Literature is, at the same time, content, strategy and didactic-pedagogical resource, as stated by Chaves (2011b) when dealing with this topic.

[1]The Research and Study Group in Early Childhood Education - GEEI is coordinated by Professor Dr. Marta Chaves, and is formalized by the State University of Maringa. This group carries out research and studies related to Early Childhood Education, based on the theoretical assumptions of Historical Materialism and from the perspective of Historical-Cultural Theory. It includes researchers from the State University of Maringa, the State University of the Midwest and the Paulista State University Julio de Mesquita Filho - Unesp, Marilia Campus; as well as academics from the undergraduate and postgraduate courses in Pedagogy at the State University of Maringa.

By studying the work of these authors, we intend to make a contribution, albeit an initial one, to the possibilities of working with the authors of literary texts for children, highlighting the work of the German authors Jacob and Wilhelm Grimm. We chose these writers because of the appreciation of their works, as well as because we were interested in learning more about their careers in children's literature and their work with the culture of their country.

In this research, we will look at biographical aspects of the Brothers Grimm, as well as their works, in order to highlight the didactic resource called Box **of Charms and Life**[2] , which can, in turn, instrumentalize the practice of teachers in order to improve teaching and enable meaningful learning for students.

Our work is bibliographical in nature and is organized as follows: initially, we will discuss the historical aspects of Children's Literature, as well as highlighting Classical Children's Literature and its authors. We will then discuss the life and works of the Brothers Grimm, in conjunction with the place and time in which the writers lived, i.e. 18th and 19th century Germany.

Next, after presenting the biographical aspects of the German authors, we will present their works, especially "Tales for Children and the Family". We will discuss the importance of Children's Literature in school educational institutions and present a proposal for pedagogical intervention through Children's Literature and working with the authors' biographies, especially that of the Brothers Grimm, with the **Box of Charms and Life**, based on the assumptions of Historical-Cultural Theory. This proposal was made because we believe that there is the possibility of working with biographies of authors in everyday school life and enriching the work of teachers who work in these educational institutions and also the teaching and learning of their students.

[2]The "Box of Charms and Life", created in 2011, is a teaching resource developed by Prof. Dr. Marta Chaves and systematized in her post-doctoral studies (CHAVES, 2011a). Dr. Marta Chaves and systematized in her post-doctoral studies (CHAVES, 2011a), which we will discuss in more detail in the course of this work.

2. HISTORICAL ASPECTS OF CHILDREN'S LITERATURE: INITIAL STUDIES

The definition of literature is very peculiar to the era in which it is written about. Coelho (2010) states that each period of history has produced its own literature, in its own way, and knowing them leads to an understanding of the uniqueness of each moment in the development of man. Knowing literature historically provides knowledge of the values on which different societies were based.

Carvalho (1982) states that it is necessary to have a concept of children in order to think about literature aimed at this audience. As Aries (2006) writes, until the 17th century, children were of no importance to society, since they were seen as miniature adults and were therefore dressed like them. Childhood, at that time, was seen as a stage of transition to adulthood, in which no special treatment was given to children.

The social transformations of the 17th century, such as the Catholic and Protestant religious reforms, helped to build a sense of childhood. They brought a new understanding of children and their learning and affection gained importance within the family, which was demonstrated by the value that education began to have. According to Aries (2006), children's learning, which used to take place when they were with adults doing their daily chores, began to take place at school from the 17th century onwards. Work for educational purposes was replaced by school, which became responsible for the training process.

Carvalho (1982) states that:

> Children and school began to take their first steps towards the sun in the 17th century, when children's literature began, although it only found its true place with the advent of the bourgeoisie, among the well-born, in the late 18th and early 19th centuries. If, for there to be written literature, two basic conditions are needed: a book and a school; for there to be children's literature, one more is added: the appeal of the child. It is on this fact that the history of

Children's Literature is based, marking its beginnings in the 17th century, the century that marks the artistic-literary calendar for children, with Perrault and Comenius (CARVALHO, 1982, p. 75).

When it comes to Children's Literature, Carvalho (1982) says that it began with Charles Perrault (1628-1703) in the 17th century, who portrayed his times in the children's stories he wrote, subtly criticizing the society in which he lived. Still in the same century, another admirable writer was Fenelon, the indocile grandson of Louis XIV, who wrote his "Te1ётасо", a veritable treatise on education.

Therefore, what we have recently come to call Children's Literature manifested itself during the 17th century, a time when changes in the structure of society had repercussions in the artistic sphere. As Carvalho (1982) points out, the emergence of this literature has its own characteristics, as it stems from the rise of the bourgeois family, the new *status* granted to children in society and the reorganization of schools.

School institutions became a legally open establishment, not only for the bourgeoisie, but for everyone in society, and Children's Literature came to confirm this process of schooling. Since "[...] Children's Literature works on written language, it depends on children's ability to read, that is, it assumes that they have passed through the school sieve" (LAJOLO and ZILBERMAN, 2004, p. 18).

The 19th century saw the start of scientific studies into the folk and popular literature of each nation, according to Coelho (1991). During this period, various studies were carried out by "[...] philologists, anthropologists, ethnologists, psychologists and sociologists who tried to detect the sources or matrix texts of this marvelous stream of literature, produced anonymously and collectively" (COELHO, 1991, p.16).

With regard to Children's Literature, Coelho (1991) states that:

> If we follow, on a journey through the texts (many of which were born centuries before Christ), we will pass through the wise and mystical regions of India or mysterious Egypt; we will confront the biblical Palestine of the Old Testament and classical Greece; we will enter the Roman Empire, discovering it as the great mediator/disseminator that was the East. At the same time, we will discover the narrative migrations that took place in Persia, Iraq, Turkey and, above all, in lustful Arabia, whose emphasis on the fullest sensorial materiality will contrast with the spiritualism generated by the dreamy imagination of the Celts and Bretons (COELHO, 1991, p. 15).

The author Nelly Novaes Coelho shows that the stories we know today, from the Middle Ages onwards, are understood by the European tradition. According to Coelho (1991), the *"cellulo mater*[1] *'* of Children's Literature, now known as classic, is to be found in Medieval Popular Novels, which have their origins in India. Coelho (1991) also argues that the most remote source of marvelous popular literature, associated with the folklore of all the nations of the western world, is the oriental one.

Today known as primordial literature, narratives also have a magical or fantastical character. In them, the fabulous background of oriental narratives has been discovered, which developed centuries before Christ and spread throughout the world through oral tradition.

The well-known classic tales, although historically they were born in 17th century France, according to Coelho (1991, p. 16) "[...] in the lavish court of King Louis XIV and by the hand of the erudite Charles Perrault", had their origins well before this period - and were born to speak to adults, as Coelho (1991) states. According to Carvalho (1982), the 18th century, with France as its birthplace, reached its magnificence in its second half. "Literature ceases to be a verbal game and becomes characterized by the search for knowledge.

Instruction was the watchword of the Enlightenment. 'The type of educator was the pedagogue'" (CARVALHO, 1982, p. 86).

As the oral tradition of storytelling is broken, the habit of reading is established; the family takes on the custom of reading to the children, abolishing the habit of sociability. "But, unfortunately, this was the privilege of the well-born children, [...] the poor unborn children displayed their misery as cleaners or janitors in the jobs that were imposed on them" (CARVALHO, 1982, p. 87).

> The eighteenth century cultivated a new genre in children's literature (more precisely, juvenile literature), but that doesn't mean that it was born in that century, [...], since it is obvious and indisputable that Perrault's tales were consecrated in the seventeenth century by all the children of the world, as well as others, such as Countess Murat, [...]; Madame D'ulnoy, [...]; to name but a few....]; Madame D'Aulnoy, [...]; to mention just the marvelous tales, which are preferred by children because they respond to their psychological structure, unlike the literature of the 18th century, whose main concern was scientific and pedagogical initiation (CARVALHO, 1982, p. 89).

According to Coelho (1991), fairy tales were not initially literature for children. This transformation began with Perrault in 17th century France, the Brothers Grimm in 18th century Germany and Andersen in 19th century Denmark.

Coelho (1980) states that alongside the collections by Perrault, La Fontaine, Grimm, Andersen and others, non-popular books were developed, called cults, which were initially aimed at adults, but ended up becoming famous as Children's or Young People's Literature.

We would point out that the first books aimed at children were created in the 17th century. According to Arroyo (1968):

> The 17th century was rich in important works for Children's Literature, but the golden age was undoubtedly the 18th century, which is intended to provide a more significant benchmark.

begins with the publication of the Brothers Grimm's collection of stories, *Kinderund Hausmarchen*[3] *in* 1812 (ARROYO, 1968, p. 30).

Carvalho (1982) considers the 18th century to be the birthplace of the great revolutions: the Industrial Revolution, on a socio-economic level, culminating in the French Revolution .[4]

According to Miranda (2012), the Industrial Revolution, followed by industrialization in the 18th century, led to the political and financial growth of cities and, consequently, the decline of rural power and feudalism. This led to the consolidation of the bourgeoisie as a social class, putting the production of European Children's Literature into context. According to Lajolo and Zilberman (2004), in its quest for political power, the bourgeoisie encouraged institutions that worked in its favor, helping it to achieve its desired goals, such as the family and the school.

Coelho (2010) writes that Children's Literature has its origins in orality is as old as human imagination. Nowadays it is understood as art, because it uses the creativity that permeates the world. (2010, p. 27), Children's Literature " fuses the dreams and practical life, the imaginary and the real, ideals and their possible and impossible realization".

In short, Children's Literature began in the 17th century, when children and schools began to organize themselves in relation to the society of the time. It was in the 18th century that children began to be considered different from adults, with their own obligations and characteristics, which is why they needed to be separated from the lives of their elders and receive a special education to prepare them for adult life.

We agree with Chaves (2011b) that it is at school that children will

---

[3] "KinderundHausmaërchen", translated into Portuguese as "Contos da Infancia e do Lar", are two books published in two editions: 1812 and 1815 by the Brothers Grimm, which contain various tales collected from the popular memory of Germany in the 18th and 19th centuries.

[4] The French Revolution is considered the great social and political movement of the 18th century. It brought the bourgeoisie to power, overthrew the feudal institutions still present in France and affected the whole of the West.

experience and learn from what is most beautiful, elaborate and advanced. We also remember that the function of education is to promote development and learning. Therefore, educational institutions should invest in good books, since Children's Literature, for us, teaches, develops and promotes interest. It is an opportunity to present and teach children meaningful human elaborations and thus make a decisive contribution to broadening the students' universe of knowledge. However, we will continue to present Classical and Contemporary Children's Literature.

2.1 CLASSIC AND CONTEMPORARY CHILDREN'S LITERATURE

According to what we have written, it was only after the 17th century that the concept of childhood began to change, when children began to be considered as such. As a result, a specific type of literature was developed for them, called Children's Literature. Before that time, children of the nobility read the great classics and the lower classes read legends and folk tales. Over time, these classics were adapted and folk tales inspired fairy tales.

Charles Perrault collected folk tales from France in the 17th century and the Brothers Grimm researched Germanic legends and tales a century later. The tales collected by these authors have been adapted and republished several times and are even altered, because, as mentioned above, the classic stories were not and are not children's stories in their origin.

According to Arroyo (1968):

> The basis of children's literature will always be oral literature, which precedes it historically and underpins it thematically. Charles Perrault took from oral tradition all the themes of his tales, subtitled Contes de maMerel'Oye[5] , a narrative of Celtic legends with roots perhaps in the East and already in the 17th century, when it appeared in his book, a common heritage throughout Western Europe (ARROYO, 1968, p. 36).

---

[5] In 1697, during the absolutist monarchy of Louis XIX , Perrault published Contes de maMerel'oye (Tales of Mother Goose). These tales were a form of literature that valued fantasy, imagination built on texts from Classical Antiquity or narratives that were present in the orality of the people (DARNTON, 1986).

Perrault introduced fantasy into Children's Literature and, according to Sandroni (1987), he made it possible for various other authors to appear with works especially aimed at children. However, during the Enlightenment[6] , due to the appreciation of rationality, stories that emphasized the presence of the marvelous were perhaps forgotten because they didn't fit in with established values, since in this period reason was valued and not the magical and marvelous. According to Coelho (2010), this historical moment favored the development of the adventure story period, which continued until the end of the 19th century.

After the French Revolution, according to Coelho (1991), the Romantic Era began, in which literary manifestations based on fantasy reappeared, with Perrault's tales becoming renowned. Also during this period, Jacob and Wilhelm Grimm began a scientific search for the mythology present in oral storytelling in Germany, collecting folk tales and various documents.

Coelho (1991) comments that more than a century separates Grimm's German tales from those recorded in France by Perrault. However, the similarities between them are obvious. Among them, the fact that these authors used the same label, fairy tales or marvelous tales, to classify their stories. The same terminology was used in relation to the tales that Andersen sought out in Nordic popular literature some twenty years after the Grimm collection (COELHO, 1991). The author adds that:

> Considered today to be the true creator of children's literature, the Danish poet and novelist Hans Christian Andersen published around two hundred *children's stories* under the general title of *Eventyr* (1835-1872). Some of them were taken from popular literature, while others were the writer's own creation. Hence the mixture of materials that coexist in his literary universe under the same label: eventyr, or, in the most common translation, "tales". (italics in the original) (COELHO, 1991, p. 76).

According to Coelho (1991), Hans Christian Andersen was the creator of

---

[6]The Enlightenment or Age of Reason (1790-1800) was a philosophical movement that appeared in France in the 18th century and advocated the use of reason as the best way to achieve freedom, autonomy and emancipation.

literature aimed at children, since he collected versions of oral tales and combined them with others from literary sources, publishing them in 1835.

Typically conveying truths and certainties, classical texts generally concentrate symbols that carry concepts, drive behavior and reinforce patterns. The classic undergoes adaptations and, "[...] with each well-executed adaptation of a classic (in various languages), a large number of readers turn to the original texts" (CECCANTINI, 2004, p. 87).

When we relate past and present, classic tales are retold by modern tales, with elements of the present day, because they convey a critique of the social values of the time; appropriating the symbolic, they represent changing attitudes in the culture.

It was from the 18th century onwards, using material from folk tales and the adaptation of classic texts and associated with schools, that Children's Literature appeared as a literary segment. Coelho (1991) analyzes that later, at the end of the 19th century, literature became critical, with several tales of an ideological nature appearing on the literary scene.

It wasn't until the 20th century that there was a concern not only with the child's intellect, but also with the child's emotional state, which led to an improvement in pedagogy and child psychology, the undisputed parameters of children's literature.

Nowadays, we can see that the reality represented in contemporary fairy tales is closer to the readers, since current fairy tales have more poetic themes that are present in everyday life, such as power relations, instability in life, the stress of the contemporary world, the duality of people, competition, questioning established values (PERROTTI, 1986).

However, the heroes, the princes, the kings and their castles revisit the tales of our day, dialoguing with them and casting an attentive and sensitive eye over them. The protagonists of contemporary stories are more active, have a voice, strength, are warriors and are hardly intimidated by danger.

Elements of classic tales are still present in contemporary tales, such as witches, princes and princesses, good and evil, castles, fairies, magic and many others. Contemporary children's literature therefore maintains a dialogue with classic tales.

2.2 EXPONENTS OF CLASSIC CHILDREN'S LITERATURE

As we mentioned earlier, the concept of Children's Literature began to expand in the 18th century. Among the classic authors of literature for children and young people were Charles Perrault, the Grimm, Andersen and others. Their texts were based on fixed, concrete places where they moved around, such as in the salons, in the social life of their time, among the people of the countryside, where they collected plenty of material with which to work on the themes in their tales.

We will present some classic authors of Children's Literature below, because, in our opinion, children should have access to the highest human elaborations and classic authors bring pleasurable moments in their tales, which bring their readers into contact with fantasy, the world of fiction, art, poetry and imagination.

The French fabulist Jean La Fontaine (1621 - 1692) gave Western literature its definitive form. According to Coelho (1985), it was in 1650 that La Fontaine began his writing career, writing plays. However, he immortalized himself with the popular literary form known as fabula. La Fontaine looked for arguments in Greek, Italian, French, Biblical parables and other readings that challenged his curiosity. What is most common among his fables is that they are "brief and instructive" (COELHO, 1985, p.61). As such, his fables became known to countless people and are still told today. Among the fables written by this classic exponent, we highlight: The Wolf and the Lamb, The Fox and the

Squirrel and The Moga and the Pail of Milk.

A 17th century French writer, Charles Perrault (1628 - 1703) was also a teacher, researcher and lawyer. According to Machado (2010), as well as being an official in Louis XIV's government, he was responsible for choosing the architects who designed the Palace of Versailles and the Louvre Museum. He entered Universal Literary History not as a classical poet, but as an author of popular literature and became known as a writer of translations.

According to Abramovich (1989), Perrault was a French academic and author of several books for adults. Despite this, he became famous and immortal for his only volume of tales for children. These were stories collected from the people, always respecting their own characteristics, such as the cruel, the moral and the poetic. He wrote versions of classic tales such as Puss in Boots, Cinderella, The Little Thumb, The Fairies and Bluebeard, for example. These narratives have taken on different forms and can be found with different elements according to the culture in which they appear. The tales of this author were simple literary adaptations that brought moral concepts into their context. Coelho (2010) points out that Perrault's tales are realistic and present a Manichaeism between the main characters.

The French novelist Jeanne-Marie Leprince de Beaumont (1711 - 1780) was a cultured lady of the luxurious French court of Louis XV. According to Machado (2010, p. 98), "[...] between 1750 and 1775 she released a series of anthologies of stories, fairy tales, essays and anecdotes". Alongside other stories, her best-known tale is Beauty and the Beast, which she published in Paris in 1757 in the book The Children's Bazaar. The author wrote her collections with the aim of instilling social virtues in children and young people.

The Germans Jacob (1785 - 1863) and Wilhelm Grimm (1786 - 1859) worked hard to determine the authentic German language, and also dedicated themselves to collecting folk tales from the regions of their country. They published two volumes of the collection Tales of Childhood and Home, in which they brought fairy tales such as Snow White, The Bremen Musicians,

Rapunzel, John and Mary, among others. According to Coelho (1991, p. 73) they were "participants in the Heidelberg Intellectual Circle [...] philologists, and great folklorists, scholars of German mythology and the history of German law".

Many of Perrault's tales were also retold by the Grimm brothers more than a century later. For Tatar (2004), the French author, unlike the German philologists, didn't try to emphasize the particular French flavour of the stories, but simply retold the tales he had heard as a child.

Danish poet and novelist Hans Christian Andersen (1805 - 1875) became famous above all for his tales which are considered masterpieces of Children's Literature. According to Machado (2010), unlike Perrault and the Grimm, Andersen claimed authorship of the stories he told, even though he admitted that some were inspired by tales he had heard as a child. According to Coelho (2010), Andersen was the author who passed on the memory of archaic texts and also invented new ones. Coelho (2003) also states that Andersen was the first authentically romantic voice to tell stories to children and suggest patterns of behavior for them to adopt. For Meireles (1984), Andersen's writings were fabulous, but only those who were part of a literate culture had access to them. His best-known works are: The Ugly Duckling, The Emperor's New Clothes, The Little Mermaid, The Princess and the Pea, The Little Matchmaker and The Snow Queen. Coelho (1985, p. 120) states that "[...] one of Andersen's peculiarities is the known mixture of 'wonder' and 'realism' in his literary material". We can see, then, that most of this author's tales feature characters, places and problems taken from people's ordinary reality.

Both the Brothers Grimm and Andersen "[...] represented in their works the pragmatic bourgeois/romantic mentality that was being consolidated at the time" (COELHO, 2010, p. 102). There is a notable difference between these authors: in the Grimm's tales, the marvelous world predominated, while in Andersen's, it is in the concrete reality of everyday life that the "marvelous" is discovered. Furthermore, the narratives collected and adapted by the German authors belonged to oral translation, while the Danish writer used two sources for his writing: popular literature preserved through oral translation or in manuscripts, and real life. Coelho (1985) points out that Andersen "invented" many more tales than his predecessors.

The English writer Charles Lutwidge Dodgson, known worldwide by his pseudonym Lewis Carroll (1832 - 1898), was the first name in the field of marvelous realism, as Coelho (1985) tells us. He was passionate about the art of photography, "[...] he was an apparently quiet man whose life was uneventful and marked by an evident love of children" (COELHO, 1985, p.126). During the reign of Queen Victoria (1838 - 1901) in England, Carroll wrote his great *work, Alice in Wonderland*, during a boat trip on the River Thames. In this book, he criticizes the customs of the civilization of his time, as Coelho (2010) states. The short story Alice in Wonderland was only published in 1865, which gave Carroll immediate notoriety. He also wrote Alice Through the Looking Glass and What Alice Found There.

The historian Joseph Jacobs (1854 - 1916) was a folklorist born in Australia who read collections of fables and fairy tales from all over the world, including British fairy tales, with a view to recovering the tradition of the people. His best-known tales include John and the Beanstalk and The Story of the Three Little Pigs.

Among so many illustrious writers of Children's Literature, we will focus on the lives of the Brothers Grimm, as they and their works are highly regarded. Therefore, we will present below historical aspects of Germany between the years 1785 and 1863, which were the years experienced by the two brothers.

3. GERMANY BETWEEN THE 18TH AND 19TH CENTURIES

Until the middle of the 19th century, Germany was divided into principalities, each with its own customs and beliefs. We'll see that this European country has a long literary tradition.

Between the 18th and 19th centuries there were many events in Germany, including the Napoleonic Wars, which consisted of a series of armed conflicts between 1799 and 1815. The general motive of the French campaigns after 1789 was to defend and spread the ideals of the French Revolution, but with the rise of Napoleon Bonaparte, the aim became the expansion of French influence and territory (FULBROOK, 2012).

At the beginning of the 19th century, Germany was conquered by the French under Napoleon. The Holy Roman German Empire[7] was abolished and in its place was created the Confederation of the Rhine, which was dissolved by the Congress of Vienna and reconstituted on new bases under the name of the German Confederation *(DeutscherBund)* in 1815.

In 1812, Napoleon defeated the Russians and conquered Moscow. However, in the retreat to Germany, the army was defeated by the cold and new conflicts broke out. Napoleon won his last major victory at the Battle of Dresden, but was forced to retreat over the Rhine after the Battle of *Leipzig*, leaving the German states free. The Russian, Austrian and Prussian armies (coalition) invaded France from the north and took Paris in March 1814. Napoleon was exiled to the island of Elba by the coalition.

As Fulbrook (2012) states, long and slow transformations took place in German society and culture at this time. Education and literacy spread, the readership expanded, new ways of thinking and questioning began to be

[7]The Holy Roman Empire was the union of territories in Central Europe during the Middle Ages, throughout the Modern and early Contemporary Ages. The empire's territorial extent varied during its history, but at its peak it encompassed the territories of the modern states of Germany, Austria, Switzerland, Liechtenstein, Luxembourg, the Czech Republic, Slovenia, Belgium, the Netherlands and much of Poland, France and Italy.

developed.

In the 18th century, Germany was a place where cultural currents flourished. The country experienced a surprising literary revival with the rebirth of German as a standard language and a vehicle for deep expression. The Enlightenment had an impact on this nation and Germany also made major contributions to classical music.

In this period, great names were revealed, such as: Immanuel Kant (1724-1804) considered one of the most notable representatives of the German enlightenment; Johann Wolfgang von Goethe (1749 - 1832), who in turn developed German literature at the time; the Grimm brothers, who were interested in the folklore of their country; Johann Sebastian Bach (1685 - 1750), Wolfgang Amadeus Mozart (1756 - 1791) and Ludwig van Beethoven (1770 - 1827), who are important composers of German classical music.

According to Fulbrook (2012, p. 110), by the end of the 18th century, Germany "[...] had established itself as the *Land der DichterundDenker* ('land of poets and philosophers')". Finally, romanticism replaced the Enlightenment, but the political structure remained shattered and the main impetus for political transformation came from the impact of the French Revolution.

As the French Revolution moved from a declaration of liberty, equality and fraternity to a regime of terror, Germany was involved, being attacked, invaded, occupied and exploited. Due to a succession of French victories, by the end of 1794 the whole of Germany west of the Rhine was under French rule. This situation lasted until 1814.

Certain political 1enбёnc1aз developed in the 1820s and 1830s, with the development of liberalism taking on more nuances and political forms than the liberalism of the 18th century.

Culturally, the period also seemed to be one of transition, as the education system continued to grow. At the lowest levels of education, the workforce produced by the German states was one of the most modern and educated in Europe. According to Fulbrook (2012), the system of idealist philosophy developed by Friedrich Hegel (1770 - 1831) would train the minds of a generation and continue to fascinate academics to this day. Among other points, Hegel saw history as a succession of stages in a process of "knowledge of the world spirit".

According to Fulbrook (2012):

> The impact of Hegel's philosophy was perhaps most important, indirectly, in its transmutation through the thought of Karl Marx (1818 - 1883), and in the subsequent development of both empirical social science and political socialism (FULBROOK, 2012, p. 126).

Marx broke with the thinking of Hegel's critics and turned Hegel's idealist philosophy on its head. Thus, Marx replaced Hegel's idealism with a new materialism, and the "world spirit" was no longer the key to historical dynamics; instead, man made his own history.

In the socio-economic field, there were transitions in social relations, production patterns and economic organization. With the transition from a feudal to a class-based society, the foundations were laid for the development of an industrial society in 1830.

In 1846 and 1847, Germany suffered from plagues on the plantations, resulting in hunger, death and misery. However, in the following year, the economy improved and social unrest broke out:

> This was not a revolutionary movement undertaken by an industrial proletariat, as envisioned in Marx's theory. The protest of the moderate working class, like that of the Berlin socialists [...] wanted trade unions, higher wages, better working conditions and the regulation of factories (FULBROOK, 2012, p.137).

In 1849 there was a disruption by the liberals and 1850 saw great economic growth with the production of textiles, iron and coal, improvements in education and the spread of faith in science and progress (FULBROOK, 2012). It was in 1871, however, that Germany really became a country, as it was in this year that it was unified.

> Bonaparte played as central a role in German history as he did in French history. Under his powerful influence, the forms of political, legal and technical-administrative existence in which Germany lived in the 19th century and, not infrequently, the 20th century were created (MANN, 1989, p. 64, apud MATA, 2006, p. 2).

Therefore, when we refer to a German "national identity", it began to take shape at a time when revolutionary France played a major role with Bonaparte and the French Revolution.

The 19th century was a period of great change for Germany, as it coincided with a unique moment in German history - the process of political unification and the formation of the Empire.

In general terms, we can say that Germany in 1815 had changed a lot from the previous century, but it was still an agricultural country, with villages, forests, princely castles and palaces and majestic churches. With the French Revolution, Germany was shaken politically, but the Industrial Revolution brought about even greater changes.

This is the historical framework that marks the youth and intellectual formation of the brothers Jacob and Wilhelm Grimm. We will now present the lives of these two great writers.

4. IRMAOSGRIMM: THEIR STORIES AND THEIR TALES

In Germany, Romantic intellectuals valued popular culture at a time when repression of it was intensifying - the end of the 18th century and the beginning of the 19th century. Among these Romantics were the Germans Jacob and Wilhelm Grimm, who began collecting tales through direct contact with peasants, driven in large part by the interest in popular traditions developed by the Romantic movement in that country and by the context of great transformations to which they belonged. Respected researchers, they also made great contributions to the German language, becoming one of the most popular and classic authors in literature.

4.1 LIFE OF TWO BROTHERS

When discussing the Grimm brothers, it is common to think that they were twins, but they are not. Jacob Ludwig Karl Grimm was born on January 4, 1785, while his brother Wilhelm Karl Grimm was born on February 24, 1786, both in the German town of Hanau (in the state of Hesse, in central Germany, near Frankfurt). They are the children of Philipp Wilhelm Grimme Dorothea Grimm. Their parents had nine children, of whom only six survived. According to Canton (2006), Jacob and Wilhelm were the eldest of the six siblings, their family was middle class and followed Calvinism.

The Grimm family has been documented as residents of Hanau since the 16th century, as restaurant owners and clergymen. Great-grandfather Friedrich Grimm was the head pastor at the Protestant St. Mary's Church *(Marienkirche)* for 42 years (BIOGRAPHICAL..., 2012).

The Grimm family lived in the city of Hanau until 1791, because it was in this year that Philip was appointed a civil servant in his hometown of Steinau in 32

Kinzing, a district of Germany, and so they moved there (BIOGRAPHICAL..., 2012). Thus, most of the siblings' childhood was spent in the village of Steinau, where their father worked as a justice and administration official for the Count of Hesse. However, in 1796, their father died and, as a result, Dorothea took over her husband's role in caring for the family until her own death in 1808.

In 1798, Jacob and Wilhelm moved to Kassel (their mother's hometown) to enter secondary school. In order to educate her children, Dorothea found support in her sister, a lady of the Kassel court, who not only ensured a livelihood for the family, but also took care of the education of her nephews. According to Grimm (2012), they studied at the *Lycée Fridericianum*, where, according to Canton (2006), Jacob and Wilhelm slept in the same bed and studied twelve hours a day, becoming the best in their class. They were marginalized by teachers and classmates because they were poorer than most of the students there.

With a lot of effort, the Grimm brothers managed to study at the University of Marburg, where they met Professor Friedrich Von Savigny, who influenced their interest in philology, German history and medieval German literature. They also met the philosopher Johann Gottfried, a forerunner of German Romanticism (MATA, 2006).It was at this university that the brothers specialized in law and philology (the broad study of language). According to Canton (2006), because they were involved in the study of literature and the customs of the people, the two began collecting tales and materials of popular origin in 1806.

It was on a trip to Paris with Professor Friedrich Von Savigny to study legal texts from the Middle Ages - about the Roman Empire - that Jacob became certain that he would not work in the field of law, but

It focuses on the literature and history of Ancient Germany, the Germanic peoples and all their mythology (GRIMM..., 2013).

For centuries, the stories known to different peoples were only transmitted orally, being told by the elders to the young. The Grimm brothers set about researching old documents and collecting tales from the German population, recording them in text in order to preserve the traditional stories of their people. As we have already mentioned, at the beginning of the 19th century, Germany was not a unified country; there was political instability, power struggles and military conquests. The Grimm wanted a consolidated nation, a spirit of unity among the people. So they began researching their native language and collecting folk tales and ancient myths, thus creating a field of research unknown at the time, preserving elements of German cultural history, which was threatened to be lost.

As Canton (2006) points out, the Grimm brothers went through countless difficulties. Wilhelm was diagnosed with asthma and had a weak heart, while Jacob, for economic reasons, went to work as Bonaparte's personal librarian in Kassel. However, despite the problems and difficulties they suffered, in 1811 Jacob published his first work: "The German Singing Masters", and Wilhelm translated old Danish legends *(Altdanische Heldenlieder).*

According to Mata (2006), Jacob Grimm paid attention to everything in popular literature that could translate the "spirit of the people". His first initiative in this field, carried out together with his brother Wilhelm, resulted in the classic *"KinderundHausmarchen",*[8] , the first edition of which was published in 1812. It is a collection of German folk tales, in which we find texts that have become classics of universal Children's Literature, such as Snow White, Rapunzel, The Frog Prince, Cinderella, John and Mary, among many others.

It was with the help of Dorothea Viehmman (an old woman from the village) that the Brothers Grimm collected some of the tales written in the *KinderundHausmarchen.* Coelho (1985, p. 110) points out that "[...] Katherina

[8] The Portuguese translation of *"KinderundHausmarchen"* is: Contos para criangas contados em casa. This work is known by various titles in Brazil, for example, Coelho (1985) presents it as "Contos de Fadas para criangas e adultos" (Fairy Tales for Children and Adults); the Cosacnaif publishing house released an edition of these tales under the title "Contos maravilhosos infantis e domesticos" (Wonderful Children's and Household Tales); Canton (2006) writes it as "Contos para criangas e para familia" (Tales for Children and the Family).

Wieckmann, a peasant with an extraordinary memory, would have been the great source of transmission for them".

The Brothers Grimm not only collected the tales, but also created them. These stories were not intended for children, but for adults. However, the brothers dedicated them to children because they were full of magical and wonderful tales. Thus, these authors managed to merge two universes that seemed very distinct: the popular and the childish (BRANDAO, 1995).

In 1819, the Grimm brothers published a revised edition of "Tales for Children and the Family", in which several tales from the first edition were deleted and new ones added. According to Grimm (2012), in the same year, Jacob began to publish his German grammar, which was not completed until 1837. They also released a translation of Irish marvelous tales in 1826.

Both became professors at the University of Gottingen, where they created the subject of Germanic studies. However, they left abruptly when they and five other professors openly protested against the dissolution of the constitution by King Ernst Augustus I, who, as a result, dismissed them and exiled three professors, including Jacob Grimm. According to Mata (2006), the Grimm were among the few in German academia at the time who accepted liberal positions. The end of this episode led to a kind of canonization of the "Gottingen Seven" in the eyes of public opinion. They came to be seen as defenders of German constitutionalism and true "heroes of the *Vormarz*"[9] .

However, it was during this period that they worked on another great work: the Great German Dictionary *(Deutsches Worterbuch),* which was the first dictionary to standardize the German language (CANTON, 2006). Only a few volumes were published while the Brothers Grimm were alive. It took generations of researchers to complete this work, which served as a model for many other dictionaries. Twenty-three years after its inception, the 32nd Dictionary was published. In 1957, the work was revised. In 1965, it was published again. In 2004, the dictionary set was released on CD-ROM. When

[9]The term *Vormarz* ("pre-March") refers to the period between 1815 and the March Revolution of 1848.

Wilhelm died, the dictionary was at letter D and when Jacob died, it was at letter F.

In 1840, the Brothers Grimm were appointed by King Friedrich Wilhelm IV of Prussia as members of the Academy of Sciences in Berlin and began working as professors at the University of Berlin (GRIMM, 2012). Jacob published a history of the German language and ended his teaching career to devote himself exclusively to scientific work. Wilhelm followed in his footsteps and retired not long after.

Over the course of their lives, the brothers took on various occupations, earning their living as librarians, journalists, diplomats and, later, teachers. But we can see that their passion was always the study of Old German and the collection of legends and fairy tales.

In 1857, "Tales for Children and the Family" reached its seventh edition. The Grimm brothers worked steadfastly until the end of their lives. Wilhelm Grimm died on December 16, 1859, at the age of 73, and his brother, Jacob, on September 20, 1863, at the age of 78. As Canton (2006) states, they are both buried in the cemetery of St. Matthaus Kirchlof, near Berlin. There is also a museum: *Bruder Grimm-Museum Kassel*, in Kassel, Germany, dedicated to these two great writers and philologists.

The city of Hanau was given the additional designation *"Brothers Grimm City*[1] ' by the Hessian Minister of the Interior and Sport in May 2006 (BIOGRAPHICAL..., 2012).The contribution of the Brothers Grimm remains little known among us. The importance of their studies undoubtedly goes beyond the linguistic-literary field. According to UNESCO's website, the tales and commentaries published by the Brothers Grimm between 1812 and 1857 have been incorporated into the Memory of the World register, an initiative designed to preserve documents and works that have marked the history of humanity.

4.2 THE WORKS AND CHARMS OF TWO GERMANS

The Brothers Grimm's first collection of tales was not published during their lifetimes. It was a manuscript containing 53 stories, some written in detail, others just sketches. This volume of fairy tales was never published, but the Grimm's interest in collecting and editing German folklore did not die.

The first edition of "Tales for Children and the Family" *(Kinderund Hausmarchen)* was published in 1812. Jacob and Wilhelm Grimm made their contribution to the German people, but above all to world culture. These tales, as already mentioned, have been recognized as a World Heritage Document by UNESCO.

As part of the popular nationalist movement in Germany due to the Napoleonic occupation, the Grimm studied the past and rediscovered the purity of popular literary sources. They published Thought, Myth, Poetry and History in 1813 and German Mythology in 1835.

They also published: "Old German Forest" *(AltdeutscheWalder)*, with 3 volumes, 1813, 1815, 1816; various writings on linguistics, folklore and medieval studies; did the translation of "The Irish Fairy Tales" *(IrischeElfenmarchen)* in 1826, wrote the introductory essay to the book "Legends and Traditions of Southern Ireland" in London, 1825.

Finally, they wrote the "Great German Dictionary" *(Deutsches Worterbuch)* which contains 32 volumes. The Grimm themselves did not finish this work; the remaining pieces were published by various generations of scholars over the years.

Of the many works written by the Brothers Grimm, we will highlight *Kinderund Hausmarchen* next, as it contains the beautiful classic tales for children and, according to Canton (2006), is the most translated and published work by these authors.

4.2.1 Tales for children and the family: tales full of fantasy

KinderundHausmarchene, according to Canton (2006), is a collection of German stories known worldwide. To make it, Jacob and Wilhelm Grimm collected more than 200 stories and translated them into literary form, a task in which Wilhelm was particularly successful. This compilation has been translated into more than 160 languages (BIOGRAPHICAL..., 2012).

According to Canton (2006), Jacob and Wilhelm Grimm collected more than 200 stories from the memory of the German people. The *Kinderund Hausmachen has been* translated into more than 160 languages (Biographical..., 2012, our translation).

People know the stories of Snow Brande, Sleeping Beauty or John and Mary. However, they probably only know them from Walt Disney's movies. What some may not know is that these and other equally famous stories were all published two hundred years ago and written down in the same book: Tales for Children and the Family.

Writing about the Brothers Grimm and retelling some of their tales, the author Katia Canton informs us that the first edition of *KinderundHausmarchen"[...]* contained not only classic fairy tales, but also magic tales, fables, legends and songs" (CANTON, 2006, p.11).

According to Tatar (2004), the Brothers Grimm, by collecting folk tales from German-speaking regions, produced a work that can be compared to the Bible in importance.When Jacob and Wilhelm Grimm developed their first plan to collect German folk tales, they wanted to capture the "pure" voice of the German people and "preserve on the printed page the oracular poetry of the common people" (TATAR, 2004, p.350).

Tatar (2004, p. 351), writing about Jacob and Wilhelm Grimm, points out that "[...] their annotations of the tales reveal the extent to which they drew on various national compilations, using literary sources and European analogues to create the definitive folkloric version of a tale". We can see that the Grimm drew on a variety of sources, both oral and literary, to put together their collection.

Coelho (1991) comments:

> In the immense mass of texts used for their linguistic studies, the Grimm rediscovered the marvelous world of fantasy and myth that had always seduced the human imagination. They selected a hundred of them and, stripping them of the erudition with which they had been treated, began to publish them under the title of *Fairy Tales for Children and Adults (KinderundHausmaerchen- 1812-1822)* (COELHO, 1991, p. 74-74, italics in the original).

Tales such as The Maiden with No Hands, The House in the Woods, The Prince and the Princess, John the Happy, among others, were written by the Brothers Grimm in the *book Kinderund Hausmaerchen* and are of German origin. Coelho (1985) states that the Grimm tales are classified as fantastical-wonderful narratives, as all the stories in this book belong to the imaginary or fantasy world. In *Tales for Children and the Family* we find teachings such as: don't accept sweets from strangers (Snow White); the important thing is not to have strength but to be clever (The Valiant Tailor); we can't promise what we can't/won't keep (The Princess and the Frog), among many others.Among the most diverse tales found in *KinderundHausmarchen,* we have chosen some titles to illustrate the vastness of their work, which we have listed in Appendix A.

December 2012 marked the 200th anniversary of the release of the first volume of the tales eternalized by the great Brothers Grimm, which contains well-known stories told to children. In the bicentenary year of the first edition of the tales in the book "Tales for Children and the Family", Cosacnaify has released the original version of 156 tales. This collection is divided into two volumes, like the original (1812 and 1815). In Germany, the bicentenary kicked off the so-called Grimm Year, an event that will run until the end of 2013 and will have as its epicenter the city of Kassel, where the two brothers have lived since 1798.

Let's stress at this point that there's no doubt that without the Brothers Grimm, stories that children know today would probably have been lost in one form or another, as well as part of German folklore.

The tales of the Brothers Grimm often reach children in adapted versions and, in many cases, teachers, parents or even the child themselves believe that this is the only true version. Below we will present TV series and films based on the tales and even on the lives of Jacob and Wilhelm Grimm, but remember that these are adapted versions and do not actually present the true stories.

4.3 GRIMM BROTHERS PRESENT IN THE ADAPTATIONS

In addition to the great works written by the Brothers Grimm themselves, we also highlight television series that use the lives of these characters and their tales as their theme.

The first series is "Grimm", from the American channel NBC, which tells the story of a detective who discovers that he is one of the last descendants of a line of captors known as Grimm (from the same family as the writing brothers). He has the ability to recognize when a person is a Wesen (creatures in the series that are half human and half animal). The Grimm are in charge of maintaining the balance between humans and Wesens.

The second is "Once Upon a Time", which takes place in the fictional town of Storybrooke. Its residents are, in fact, fairytale characters who have been sent to the real world through a curse placed on them by Snow White's Queen Ma. The only hope lies with Emma Swan, who was taken from the fairytale world before she could be cursed. As such, she is the only person who can break the curse and restore the memories of the lost characters, aided by her son, Henry, who has a book of fairy tales that holds the key to ending the curse. Some of the main characters are from the Grimm Brothers' tales, such as Snow White and Queen Ma, Rumpelstiltskin, Little Red Riding Hood and her grandmother. They also mention the tales of John and Mary, Cinderella and Sleeping Beauty.

We also remember the episode *Bedtime Stories*, from the series "Supernatural", where Sam and Dean Winchester investigate a town that has been affected by strange murders reminiscent of fairy tales such as Little Red Riding Hood and John and Mary.

There are also several films inspired by the tales of the Brothers Grimm, such as Snow White and the Huntsman (Universal Pictures, 2012), Mirror Mirror Mine (Imagem Filmes, 2012), The Girl in the Red Cloak (Warner Bros, 2011), John and Mary (Paramount Pictures, 2013), the animations Tangled (Walt Disney Pictures, 2010) inspired by the tale of Rapunzel and The Princess and the Frog (Walt Disney Pictures, 2009) motivated by the tale of The Frog Prince.

We also note that the brothers themselves were given a movie in 2005, entitled *The Brothers Gr/mm*. In it, the Grimm made a living by taking advantage of popular belief in Medieval Europe - Jacob, who is very shy and has a vivid imagination, lives in the hope that magic exists and Will doesn't believe in it, but makes the most of his fame to get women and money, as the synopsis of the movie says. They create fantastical myths and apply theatrical tricks to make them come true, so they are called upon to put an end to witches and ghosts that they themselves have invented. In the course of the movie, some of the German brothers' fairy tales, such as: Little Red Riding Hood, Frog Prince, Sleeping Beauty, John and Mary, Rapunzel and Cinderella appear to be part of the adventure.

In addition, according to Moraes (2013), the Brothers Grimm were part of the plot of the Rio de Janeiro samba school "Unidos da Tijuca" in 2013, which talked about the time of the Brothers Grimm and high technology. In this carnival parade, the honoree was Germany. One of the school's sections was dedicated to the German influence on the arts, with its strong presence in classical music, cinema and literature. In this section, references were made to Beethoven's symphonies, the drama created by Bertold Brecht and Goethe's literature. Next, the Brothers Grimm were remembered with their fairy tales on a float featuring the authors' characters, such as Snow White and John and Mary.

So far, we have revealed the greatness of the Brothers Grimm for the 21st century. Their classic tales have been re-adapted for the cinema. Their characters are and will forever be known, both for the original tale and for the various adaptations they have undergone.

5. CHILDREN'S LITERATURE AND CULTURAL-HISTORICAL THEORY

When we talk about the so-called children's classics by Perrault, Grimm or Andersende, we have to remember that they were writers who were interested in the folklore of their people and transcribed it, as Coelho (1985) writes.

Children's tales are directly embedded in culture, even through oral transmission. They are also inserted without social class distinctions and take on popular connotations, just as Burke describes:

> The idea of popular culture or Volkskultur originated in the same place and at the same time as cultural history: in Germany at the end of the 18th century. Folk songs and tales, dances, rituals, arts and crafts were discovered by middle-class intellectuals at the time. However, the history of popular culture was left to antique lovers, folklorists and anthropologists. It was only in the 1960s that a group of historians, mainly but not exclusively English-speaking, began to study it (BURKE, 2008, p.29).

In view of the above, we would like to state that Children's Literature is an instrument and a space where the learning of daily practices can and does take place, containing strategies and rules of culture of a given society.Meireles (1984) states that Literature is a broad intellectual activity, it goes beyond everything that is written, because it needs to rely on the imagination of those who read, in addition, the interpretation of words is necessary.

Through our supervised curricular internships and our work in some school institutions, we have observed that work with children's literature is currently taking a back seat. We see educational programs that are not very capable of bringing children closer to literature and culture, presenting fragmented literary texts in order to fit into the space of the textbook, generating an approximation of the beginning with the end, as well as often having their endings altered.

Abramovich (1989) writes:

> It is by listening to stories that one can feel (also) important emotions, such as sadness, anger, irritation, well-being, fear, joy, dread, insecurity, tranquillity and so many others, and deeply experience everything that the narratives provoke in those who listen to them - with all the breadth, significance and truth that each of them has (or hasn't) brought out... It is listening, feeling and seeing with the eyes of the imagination (ABRAMOVICH, 1989, p. 17).

With the above in mind, we believe that Children's Literature needs to be worked on well, since it can contribute to the formation of character and the general formation of the child as a critical and well-informed person, in other words, from the perspective of humanization.It is through Children's Literature that the development of human abilities such as creation, language and imagination can be made possible, as well as presenting possibilities for teaching methods and resources that are fundamental to the realization of educational practices, with which educators and children can have access to the human riches elaborated at different historical moments. For, as Leontiev (1979) puts it:

> Specifically human aptitudes and traits are in no way transmitted by biological heredity, but are acquired in the course of life through a process of appropriation of the culture created by previous generations (LEONTIEV, 1979, p. 285).

Just as these psychic capacities are external to the subject at birth, in order for them to be adapted and developed to more elaborate levels, the right conditions of life, education and activity are important.

Mukhina (1996) points out that:

> The different conditions in which a child's psychological development takes place interfere in different ways. The natural conditions - the constitution of the organism, its functions and its maturation - are essential; without them there can be no psychic development, but they do not determine the child's psychic qualities. That depends on living conditions and education, under the influence of which the child assimilates social experience.
>
> Social experience is the source of the child's psychic development; it is from there, with the adult as mediator, that the child receives the material with which the psychic qualities and properties of his personality will be built (MIKHINA, 1996, p. 43).

It is therefore essential to plan and organize activities through which children can learn to use these abilities. Vygotsky (2009) states that the cultural world, unlike the natural world, is the fruit of imagination, since "[...] fantasy is not opposed to memory" (VIGOTSKI, 2009, p. 23). He also explains that imagination is nourished by material experienced by the person. On this basis, we agree with Vygotsky that the richer the human experience, the greater the material available to imagination:

> The creative activity of imagination depends directly on the richness and diversity of a person's previous experience, because this experience constitutes the material with which the constructions of fantasy are created (VIGOTSKI, 2009, p. 22).

With this in mind, we believe that by working with Children's Literature, we can broaden children's cultural experience and develop their creative capacity. We understand that Children's Literature is not restricted to stories; it is poetry, music and stories in the most varied forms of expression and popular register. The use of these resources in Children's Literature allows us to meet "[...] one of the precepts of the Historical-Cultural Theory and we would, in essence, establish a full education for those who teach and for those who need to learn" (CHAVES, 2011b, p. 98).

This statement tells us that literature can be a resource for full and exceptional education, in other words, it is a way of introducing children to the most elaborate knowledge. Leontiev (1979) argues that it is through contact with the knowledge already developed by previous generations that the child will be able to develop as a man, in a process of hominization. Thus, human productions must be inherited by all.

We argue that Children's Literature is fundamental to children's development, such as orality, imagination, writing, contact with others and with different types of art. We point out that the teacher's mediation with the students in their first contact with books is essential. Strategies are needed to ensure that literature is effective in the educational process, i.e. it is important to introduce children to what humanity has produced, as this will guarantee the possibility of developing their higher psychological functions.

For Historical Cultural Theory, the educator's role is to mediate the child's relationship with the world in which he or she is inserted, in order to bring about advances that would not happen without pedagogical intervention. As Vygotskyi (1988) points out, good teaching - empowering education - is that which, by getting ahead of development, makes the child advance to ever higher levels. This being the case, we believe that the pedagogical intervention proposal devised and created by Professor Dr. Marta Chaves, the Box for Children, is a good example of this. Marta Chaves, the **Box of Enchantment and Life**, can be a teaching resource that offers children quality content and that actually humanizes them, and can help teachers in the teaching and learning process of their students.

The **Box of Enchantment and Life** was systematized to develop human abilities such as imagination, creation, memory, language and creativity, based on Historical Cultural Theory.

6. THE GRIMM BROTHERS' BOX OF CHARMS AND LIFE - A POSSIBILITY FOR TEACHING AND LEARNING WITH ENCHANTMENT

It is at school that literary studies should be privileged, where the exercise of the mind should be stimulated. As Coelho (2010, p. 16) states, "[...] school today is the privileged space in which the foundations for the formation of the individual should be laid", in other words, it is in this environment that teachers need to instigate children to appreciate reading, art and the most advanced and beautiful things.

Abramovich (1989) points out that listening to stories (children's first contact with written text) is the beginning of a learning process that can turn them into voracious readers. It is in this sense that we believe that the Box of **Charms and Life is** an instrument that encourages the development of curiosity, as well as being a teaching resource.

The **Box of Charms and Life**, being a teaching resource, has elements that need to be carefully considered. This method is duly elaborated and organized as a pedagogical intervention as the studies are refined. When this resource was created, it took as its starting point the classic elaborations of Historical-Cultural Theory, particularly in the writings of Vygotsky (2009) and Leontiev (1979), among other classic studies of the theory.

As we have already seen, this tool has been systematized with an eye to human abilities - imagination, creation, memory, language and creativity. We also believe that the **Box of Charms and Life** can broaden the vocabulary and cultural universe of children and teachers. But first and foremost, what we want to teach the children needs to be learned and appreciated by the teachers.

Vygotsky (2009) affirms the importance of teaching art, since the human condition of the child can be enhanced as much as its creativity. It is therefore necessary to return to the essentiality of organization. The teacher must plan the activities and be aware of the time and environment in which the children will be.

Therefore, "[...] the more humanity progresses, the richer the socio-historical practice it has accumulated, the more the specific role of education grows and the more complex its task" (LEONTIEV, 1979, p. 273). In other words, offering students in nursery or elementary school contact with the biographical data of an exponent of Children's Literature means understanding that, from school age onwards, children need access to more elaborate knowledge in order for their psychic functions to develop.

Through the **Box of Enchantment and Life**, students can play and learn with the stories and characters, following the guidelines of Mukhina (1996) who reaffirms that when children come into contact with the arts, they establish comparisons, make impressions, interpret conflicts and consider different hypotheses.

Chaves (2011a) points out that:

> Working with young children must be made possible from a perspective of humanization and emancipation, in which teaching procedures are rich in meaning, affection and communication. In this respect, the choice of resources and procedures are essential features of the teaching process (CHAVES, 2011a, p.56).

In other words , you can 't present biographical data in the following way impoverished, because our historical condition allows us to rely on resources such as the **Box of Enchantment and Life** which, in turn, had a wide content and allows the teacher to build many relationships with the students.

6.1 MAKING THE CHARM AND LIFE BOX

The **Box of Enchantment and Life** is a teaching resource developed by Professor Dr. Marta Chaves, in which specific elements and foundations are written in her post-doctoral work. We can announce that it was developed collectively and with the effective participation of teachers and children who chose an exponent of literature, music, poetry or the plastic arts to be studied. Its aim is to present and teach children and students in general the highest human achievements, a fundamental proposition of Historical Cultural Theory.

The **Charms and Life Box** has a form of composition that needs to be strictly adhered to, just like any other resource. The term "charms" is not gratuitous, but because it really needs to be. First of all, it must be made of wood, because, among other things, it is more durable. The illustration or external composition must have an immediate relationship with aspects relating to the life of the chosen exponent, and not to a particular work. In its composition, the Box presents five themes: family, life, works, characters and curiosities. It can include photographs, objects, texts and other varied resources (such as miniature musical instruments), which reflect the "charms" of the chosen exponent.

Our proposal for a pedagogical intervention in this work is the creation of one of these Boxes of literary exponents.
chosen were the classic "Brothers Grimm" authors. Once the exponent to be mentioned has been chosen, it is very important to carry out detailed research on him, which will support the preparation of the **Box of Charms and Life.** In other words, every **Box of Charms and Life** should have a research and study box, which will contain all possible and imaginable research on the exponent. At the end of the research, it will be possible to choose which elements of the life and work are relevant and will be highlighted in the 50th edition.

execution of the material. Among the elements found, it will be possible to choose aspects such as life, family, works, characters, friends, travels, among others. In this case, we will refer to five of these items, which will become, in the composition of the box, bags, envelopes or something similar that can contain information about the author. As well as research, to make the contents of the **Box of Charms and Life** more meaningful, it's important to include photos relating to the theme and objects that might remind you of the exponent.

To make the **Box of Enchantment and Life of** the Brothers Grimm, after the research, we chose to make fabric envelopes with the following themes: life, works, tales, adaptations and tributes (Appendix B). Inside each of these envelopes you'll find the research data for each of these themes, duly referenced, with photos and objects that may be related to the exponent and the theme dealt with (Appendix C), ensuring harmony.

According to Machado (1999), the best stimulus for reading is curiosity, so the **Box of Charms and Life** should suggest curiosity and, of course, relate to the author being studied. By having contact with the **Box of Charms and Life**, the child will see, touch, hear, ask and feel about the biography of an exponent of Children's Literature. This will be significant enough to arouse their interest in learning more about that author and their works. In order to do this, the pupil must carry out some initial reading and research, even if only briefly, in order to develop their curiosity which, in turn, is a higher psychological function.

Therefore, according to the writings presented here, we believe that the study of Children's Literature and the development of the teaching resource **Box of Enchantment and Life** offers the possibility of contributing to learning and enchantment for all children. Next, we'll present our final thoughts on this initial study.

7. FINAL CONSIDERATIONS

In this study, we briefly analyze reflections on Children's Literature and its importance in Early Childhood Education. To do this, we used authors who write about the historical aspects of Children's Literature. It is part of every human being's life, but sometimes it is not as well exposed as it should be, but it is up to educators to ensure excellent education for all and to provide the best that humanity has produced.

In this text, we assess that literature, used by educators to instigate curiosity, leads children to question, hypothesize, argue and compare the content of stories with their own experiences. We argue that literature is a human elaboration resulting from the historical and social context of its authors. In this way we can understand that it is part of the knowledge historically accumulated by men and is characterized by being one of the expressions of art. As such, it deserves great importance when we think about presenting quality Children's Literature in educational institutions.

To this end, we have provided biographical information on the writers Jacob and Wilhelm Grimm, focusing on historical aspects, their experiences, their works and their classic tales from German memory. As we can see, the Brothers Grimm were a big name in Children's Literature worldwide, since their tales were written between the 18th and 19th centuries and are known, retold and adapted to this day.

We believe that the teaching resource, **Caixa de Encantos e Vida**, is understood as a means of enriching contact with literature in the pedagogical interventions carried out by teachers. Exploring the material in a wide-ranging way can provide children with greater and more enjoyable contact with literature and its authors. However, the **Box of Enchantments and Vida** is a resource that reaffirms the importance of school as a space and time for the appropriation of knowledge and the appreciation of art.

Therefore, by presenting Children's Literature to children, we will be proposing greatness to them, teaching them what is most advanced and beautiful, developing sensitivity, as in the story Snow White, by the Brothers Grimm, as well as encouraging and promoting interest and curiosity, as in the stories The Bremen Musicians and Rumpelstiltskin, also by Jacob and Wilhelm Grimm.

Finally, we would like to emphasize that in order to implement this idea, it is necessary to train teachers to reflect on these supports and on the possibility of developing resources such as the one presented here, since initial training is only the basis for improving knowledge. Therefore, we would like to emphasize the importance of the experiences of the Group of Studies and Research in Early Childhood Education (GEEI), which provide us with moments of training such as this one in the development of the **Box of Enchantment and Life** and help us to think of strategies for developing enchanting learning in children.

REFERENCES

ABRAMOVICH, F. **Literatura Infantil**: Gostosuras e Bobices. Sao Paulo: Scipione, 1989.

ARIES, P. **Historia social da crianga e da familia**. Rio de Janeiro: LTC, 2ª ed., 2006.

ARROYO, L. **Brazilian Children's Literature.** Sao Paulo: Melhoramentos. 1968.

BRANDAO, A. A **presenga dos Irmaos Grimm na Literatura Infantil e no folclore Brasileiro**. - Sao Paulo: IBRASA, 1995.

BIOGRAPHICAL milestones of the Brothers Grimm.**Deutsche MarchenStrabe**. 2012. Available at <http://www.deutsche-maerchenstrasse.com/en/brothers-grimm/biographical-milestones-of-the-brothers-grimm/>Accessed on: August 27, 2013.

BURKE, P. **What is cultural history**? Rio de Janeiro: Jorge Zahar 2008.

CANTON, K. **Once upon a time, Brothers Grimm** - Sao Paulo: DCL, 1st ed, 2006.

CARVALHO, B. V. de. **Children's literature**: **a** historical and critical view. 2.ed. Sao Paulo: Edart, 1982.

CECCANTINI, J. L. T. **The adaptation of the classics**. The reading wheel. Sonia Aparecida Lopes Benites and Rony Farto Pereira (Org.). Sao Paulo: Cultura Academica; Assis: ANEP. 2004.

CHAVES, M. **The formation and education of the young child**: Vygotsky's studies on art and his contributions to pedagogical practices for early childhood education institutions. Araraquara, 2011a. Post-doctoral work at the Faculty of Sciences and Letters of Araraquara, Paulista State University Julio de Mesquita Filho (Unesp), under the supervision of Prof. Dr. Newton Duarte.

CHAVES, M. Links between Historical-Cultural Theory and children's literature. In: CHAVES, M. (Org.). **Praticas pedagogicas e literatura infantil**. Maringa: Eduem, 2011b, p. 97-106. (Col. Formagao de Professores, EAD, n. 44).

COELHO, N. N. **Children's Literature**. Sao Paulo: Quiron, 1980.

COELHO, N. N. **Panorama historico da literatura infantil e juvenil**. Sao Paulo: Quiron, 1985.

COELHO, N. N. **The fairy tale**. Sao Paulo: Atica. 1991.

COELHO, N. N. **Literatura infantil:** teoria, analise, didatica. 1. ed. Sao Paulo: Moderna, 2010.

COELHO, N. N. **The fairy tale**: symbols, myths, archetypes. Sao Paulo: DCL, 2003.

DARNTON, R. **O grande massacre de gatos, e outros episodios da historia cultural francesa**. Rio de Janeiro: Graal, 1986.

FULBROOK, M. **Concise History of Germany**. Translated by Barbara Duarte. Sao Paulo: Edipro, 2012.

GRIMM, J. and GRIMM, W. **Wonderful tales for children and households** / introduction Marcus Mazzari; translation Christiane Rohrig; illustration J. Borges. - Sao Paulo: Cosacnaify, 2012.

GrimmpatriaNorthHesse. Available at <http://www.grimm2013.nordhessen.de/en/marburg>. Accessed on: August 1, 2013.

LAJOLO, M; ZILBERMAN, R. **Literatura Infantil Brasileira**: historia & historias. 6 ed. Sao Paulo. Atica, 2004.

LEONTIEV, A. Man and culture. In: **O desenvolvimento dopsiquismo**. Lisbon: Livros Horizonte, 1979. p. 200-284.

MACHADO, A. M. **Contracorrente**: conversas sobre leitura e política. Sao Paulo: Atica, 1999.

MACHADO, A. M. **Fairy tales**: by Perrault, Grimm, Andersen & others / introduction by Ana Maria Machado; translation by Maria Luiza X. de A. Borges. - Rio de Janeiro: Zahar, 2010.

MATA, S. and MATA, G. Os irmaos Grimm entre romantismo, historicismo e folcloristica. **Revista Fenix**, Uberlandia, v. 3, n. 2, 2006.

MEIRELES, C. **Problemas da literatura infantil**. 3.ed. Rio de Janeiro: Nova Fronteira, 1984.

MIRANDA, F. S. M. P. The Changing Economic Paradigm, the Industrial Revolution and the Positivization of Labor Law. **Electronic Journal Direito, Justiga e Cidadania**, Sao Paulo, v. 3, n. 1, 2012.

MORAES, P. **Unidos da Tijuca takes "enchanted Germany" to the Sambodromo**. 2013. Available at: <http://www.dw.de/unidos-da-tijuca-leva-a-alemanha-encantada-para-o-samb%C3%B3dromo/a-16582583> Accessed on 04 Mar 2013.

MUKHINA,V. **Psychology of the Preschool Age**. Trad. Claudia Berliner. Sao Paulo: Martins Fontes, 1996.

PERROTTI, E. **The seductive text in children's literature**. Sao Paulo: Icone, 1986.

SANDRONI, L. **De Lobato a Bojunga**: as reinagoes renovadas. Rio de Janeiro: Agir, 1987.

TATAR, M. **Fairy tales**: commented and illustrated edition. Edition, introduction and notes by Maria Tatar; translation by Maria Luiza X. de A. Borges. Rio de Janeiro: Zahar, 2004.

UNESCO. **Die Kinder- undHausmarchen der Bruder Grimm**. 2012. Available at: <http://www.unesco.de/mow-hausmaerchen.html>Accessed on: 07 May 2013.

VIGOTSKII, L. S. Learning and development at school age. In: VIGOTSKII, L. S.; LURIA, A. R.; LEONTIEV, A. N. **Language, Development and Learning**. Sao Paulo, Icone: Edusp, 1988. p. 103-117.

VIGOTSKI, L. S. **Imagination and creation in childhood** (Translation by Zoia Prestes). Sao Paulo: Atica, 2009.

APENDICES

APPENDIX A - SOME TALES FOUND IN THE BOOK: *KINDER UND* HAUSMARCHEN BY THE GRIMM BROTHERS (VOLUME I AND II, COSACNAIFY PUBLISHING HOUSE - 2012)

1. *The frog king or Iron Henry.*
2. *Cat and mouse in society.*
3. *Mary's protégé.*
4. *Good bowling and card games.*
5. *The wolf and the seven little goats.*
6. *The nightingale and the blind snake*.
7. *The stolen coins.*
8. The hand with the knife.
9. The twelve brothers.
10. Bunch of rags.
11. Little brothers and sisters.
12. Rapunzel.
13. The three little men in the forest.
14. The damn linen spinning.
15. John and Mary.
16. Mr. Done and Done.
17. The white snake.
18. The journey of straw, hot coals and beans.
19. The fisherman and his wife.
20. The brave tailor [I and II].

21. Cinderella.

22. When they were children they played tag [I and II].

23. The mouse, the bird and the tongue.

24. The three crows.

25. Little Red Riding Hood.

26. Death and the goose herder.

27. The bone that sings.

28. Lice and fleas.

29. Amoga without hands.

30. Wise John [I and II].

31. Ogato in boots.

32. John's doctrine.

33. The sparrow and its four chicks.

34. Dona Raposa [I and II].

35. The bandit groom.

36. The best man.

37. The andangas of Little Thumb.

38. Sleeping Beauty.

39. Snow White.

40. Rumpelstilzchen.

41. The golden egg.

42. A thousand skins.

43. The king and the lion.

44. The carnation.

45. The mother-in-law.

46. The fox and the geese.

47. Poor and rich.

48. Ognomo .

49. The genius of the bottle .

50. Frog prince .

51. The crows.

52. The old woman in the forest.

53. The three brothers

54. The lion and the frog.

55. The blue light.

56. The king's two sons.

57. The iron stove.

58. The fox and the horse.

59. My shoes are worn out from all the walking .

60. The six servants.

APPENDIX B - COMPOSITION OF THE BOX OF CHARMS AND LIFE

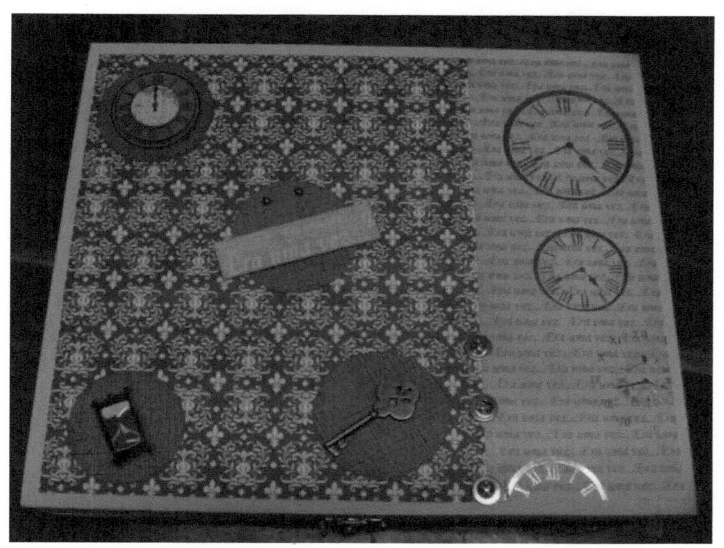

Figure 1 and 2: Box of Charms and Life of the Brothers Grimm - external view

Figure 3: The Brothers Grimm's Box of Charms and Life - Inside the box, also duly painted

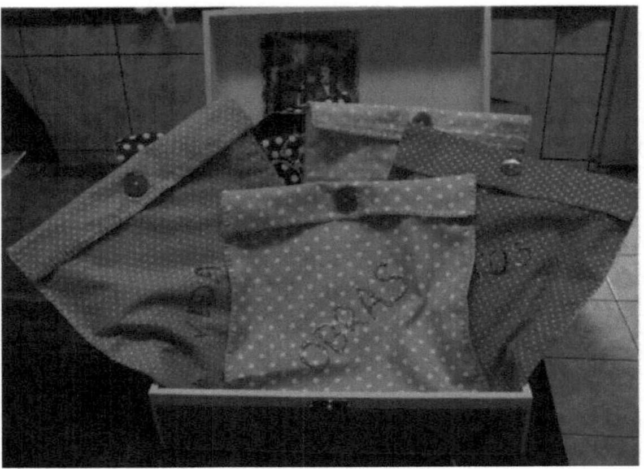

Figure 4: Box of Charms and Life of the Brothers Grimm - Envelopes with the themes

APPENDIX C - COMPOSITION OF THE ENVELOPES THAT MAKE UP THE BOX OF CHARMS AND LIFE

Figure 5: Box of Charms and Life of the Brothers Grimm - Life: contains data and images of the writers from childhood to adulthood

Figure 6: Box of Charms and Life of the Brothers Grimm - Works: contains information and photos of the works made by Jacob and Wilhelm Grimm

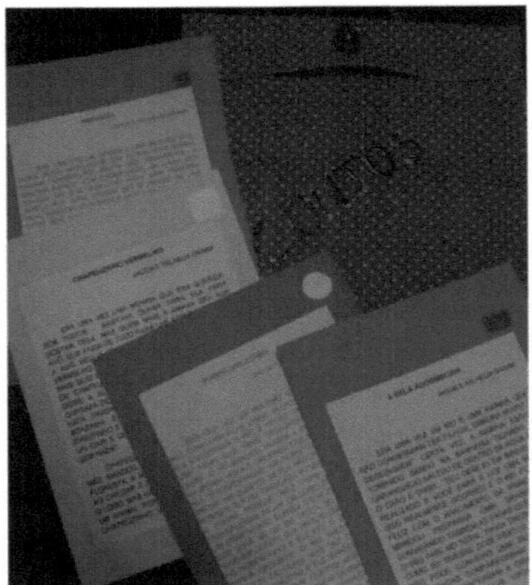

Figure 7: Box of Charms and Life of the Brothers Grimm - Tales: contains the transcription of some of the Brothers Grimm's tales, written in "Tales for Children and the Family".in "Tales for children and families"

Figure 8: Box of Charms and Life of the Brothers Grimm - Adaptations: images from films and TV series based on the tales and lives of Jacob and Wilhelm Grimm

Figure 9: Box of Charms and Life of the Brothers Grimm - Tributes: data and photos from museums, statues honoring the Brothers Grimm

COLLECTION: Prof. Dr. Marta Chaves, State University of Maringa, 2013.

I want morebooks!

Buy your books fast and straightforward online - at one of world's fastest growing online book stores! Environmentally sound due to Print-on-Demand technologies.

Buy your books online at
www.morebooks.shop

Kaufen Sie Ihre Bücher schnell und unkompliziert online – auf einer der am schnellsten wachsenden Buchhandelsplattformen weltweit! Dank Print-On-Demand umwelt- und ressourcenschonend produzi ert.

Bücher schneller online kaufen
www.morebooks.shop

info@omniscriptum.com
www.omniscriptum.com

MIX
Papier aus verantwortungsvollen Quellen
Paper from responsible sources
FSC® C105338

Printed by Books on Demand GmbH, Norderstedt / Germany